The Fiction of Flying

The Fiction of Flying

Wing Yau

Puncher & Wattmann

First published in 2026
Published by Puncher and Wattmann
PO Box 279
Waratah NSW 2298

https://www.puncherandwattmann.com
web@puncherandwattmann.com

ISBN 9781923099647

Cover image: 'Carwoola' by Miranda Douglas
Cover design by Miranda Douglas
Typesetting by Morgan Arnett
Printed by Lightning Source International

A catalogue record for this work is available from the National Library of Australia

Contents

Part I The ~~Self-Stamped~~ Passport

Part II The ~~Unreturning~~ Boomerang

Part III A ~~Lonely~~ Paper Airplane

Appendix

I

The ~~Self-Stamped~~ Passport

Rooftop Chicken (Fiction of Flying)

"No one will believe this story I'm telling, so it must be true."
Sherman Alexie

My grandma said in the fiction of flying
everyone knows about the rooftop chicken.
They used to live on the top floor of buildings
in a place known as the Pearl of the Orient,
before its beauty was pilfered
by the Symphony of Light –

or so it's remembered. Each time the chicken hopped
from one building to the next, their wings spread,
such was the pretext of flying on rooftop.
A mottled feather floated like an aria flowed
out of the prostitute's window – a reward for us
who worked hard and dreamed with our heads low.
"It's a symbol of good luck, if the feather got stuck
to your back on your way home." But

Someone bridged the gaps between buildings
with power and concrete. The chicken now walked
from one roof to the next. Down in the wet alley
we still worked hard – washing dishes with sweat
and digging endless holes on dead-end roads .

Half intoxicated in the sunless heat
I asked my grandma about the chicken.
"They were chased away by the pheasants.
One by one they plunged off the concrete heaven,
eaten and forgotten." But how did the other
birds get up there in the first place?
Even my grandma did not know.

Don't Give the Lazy Immigrant Flowers

After Ouyang Yu

The world is full; you and I are just strangers.
But at least this park is empty. I walk
on the left and don't need to make way
for anyone's purpose. Aimless,
I'm at my lazy immigrant pace.

A fortune-teller once said it takes on average
a year for an average immigrant to get a job.
It took me two. They interviewed me & my deft
fingers for data entry. I said I am bilingual;
have lived in three countries, and love
poetry. They nodded. "What else?" I can multitask.
They shrugged. "All women can," they said.

The lazy immigrant has nothing to lose
in the woman's world of administration,
doing a woman's work. Women talk about
Sheike, tousled hair, and comfy shoes.
I am too lazy to listen. A task well done
means sometimes we get to bring home
a bouquet of flowers — a reward from the boss
who says my name is hard to remember.

I, the lazy immigrant, work hard
but flowers have no place at home
or in this park where white ibis and pigeons scavenge
next to the Confucius statue.
Just like this swollen world has no place
for the three alphabets I've earned

to put after my name — I remove them
from my résumé, and drop them in a tree's crevasse,
next to a startled possum — the way I've seen
it done in a Wong Kar Wai film years ago.

Here, gnarled trees steel their sere backs
and let their crowns roar louder than wind.
Not fluent in English, their voice is often mistaken
as the soppy sound of self-pity. It's Sunday,
and I am too lazy to commiserate.

Hard to Think

Sweaty hair sticks to his forehead
as he sings with the muted ad on TV.
His lips sync with the screaming next door,
a human soundscape in Tagalog.
It is hard to think here, those he has
left behind: a room on Queen's Road,
slithers of the Victoria Harbour
between high-rises. People like him always
say they come here for a better life.

The corniced ceiling incongruent
with its unrelenting peeling plaster –
a fungal disease at the centre.
Underneath, square holes for air
blocked by dead insects. When wind
blows how many upturned bodies
will it take to make a chorus for the home-
coming concert? It's hard to think.

Taped on the wall,
above where his head lies every night
a poster of an unsmiling woman –
Her glossy honeyed back smooth
like a tune he hums in the shower.
Her face half-turned,
seducing no one in particular.
He spends more time studying
the trapped spider somewhere at the corner
of the wall than missing the women at home.
He finds it hard to think back –

To his left, the heel of yesterday barely scuffs
the wooden floorboard as it makes its way
to the back door. It sounds, he thinks,
like a yawn of a polite host.

All the Names

It's not everyday you get to enunciate
each consonant and vowel
to their mispronounced fate.

The Sze, the Rueng, or Sone, or Zhan,
or Ng, jobless in the room, all refuse to be
the monosyllabic sound you just made.

You clink a herbal lozenge
against your front teeth to make an entrance,
puffed cheeks show moxie of a public servant.

Next, you put on a bored face which is
a work face which is the face that makes the cover
of a customer service handbook. You ask:

"Ho, have you been looking for a job in the past fortnight?"
"Do you have any income to report, Ho?"
You imagine her friend saying "Hi, Ho!" but your bored
face is professional so Ho knows you mean business.

Once a Wing sat across from you, in an afternoon much like
this one that'd made you crave to carve a work song
under the desk. Out of work, despite the wing. What if Wing

is WingWing? How about Wings?
If names have Siamese twins can they
split into win-win situations?

You shake your head to file away that chuckle
and blink idly at your own chest, which sat
just above a stack of paperwork you named

Marvel, or Marvy. You make new names for your future
children, backyard birds and trees. All the names
that loll with scattered options and languor built in.

The Appraisal

i.
What does it mean to be here
mopping and wiping down
handrails all day? To be
here and not, say, out
there, where you have to speak
English and have everything
done by the book?

What the boss really wants
to ask his cleaner
in the mid-year appraisal is
How happy are you here.

He thinks *here* means Australia
and he nods like an Australian: *Here*
is great. I play
the erhu *sitting on a crate*
next to the traffic light.
My rusty mooncake tin
a sweet spot for the sound
of gold coins
splashing down...

ii.
The boss is used to hearing
forced praises during appraisals.
He takes a sip of tea
and waits.
The cleaner misreads
his extended pinkie
as a sign of approval
& emits a mimicry
of a glissando,
out of tune and practice —

Dust whirls
with excessive vowels
from his mother tongue.
A broken raconteur's verse:
"I've come here —
"... a better life — "

iii.
A fly applauds
on a green Mento
wrap his boss
expects him to clean up
after the appraisal.
The room is now expanding
into a fat universe of boss's
tenor, misty with sugary saliva.
The cleaner focuses on the fish
he will buy to steam
for dinner tonight.
His wife, at home
playing Bingo online,
will be happy. They both love
fish. Love how their mouths
and eyes are opened,
full of blankness and ice.

Sweat, like suspended time
in all conference rooms worldwide,
slowly drips as he straightens
his sore back.

On Post-Victory Day

Australia said "yes" to marriage equality on 15 Nov, 2017

Dear Father,

Who hides in the kitchen, whose name
I carry like an idle onomatopoeia
for small triumph. But whom I don't love
enough. On the day of our victory,
let's ask ourselves: what if it is true
that fathers and daughters were lovers
in their past lives? I still remember
the Stephen King book you gave me
when I was 10. I have learned
horror stories and growing up
have only one thing in common.
Winning is difficult in life, as you sat there
imparting useless information
as if they were lip service to survive.
Tears glistened on your face —
oily, like mine, you confessed:
I never knew what it was like
to have a mother.
The sob so shrill it sunders
our catoptric worlds.
I've since found power in the feminine,
such as screaming, and practise
widening my too-round eyes.
I began to see ghosts
on my pillow — the mythical
fiery shadows of Phoenix
leaping from a hot pan
to boiling water reliving a past.

In your hand a Chinese fairy tale,
some fiction about flying,
in which there is your name:

Wai Wing (Great Prosperity).

Your masculinity a carapace —
what are you made of
by the way, when Ma bought you
pink sanitary pads
instead of the blue ones
you need as a man?
You only said your knees hurt
on your way to the post office
to vote No. Now I see,
your porcelain heart
has a leaking hole. I, too,
nearly broke my body
just to savour the line
segment in my flattened world.
That's why I have your nose, your taste
for bitter tea and the will to flaunt
courage with mild hypochondria.
Out there, they have debated love and
how to be a man or a woman
is next. In my dream, the world
changes in no one's favour.
I'm playing the piano,
my hand pauses in mid air:
a semibreve. Musical notes
twirl dully in the dark, like
embroidery coming undone —
it's the crossed stitches of Phoenix,

the most unloved childhood emblem
sutured on my pillowcase.

The Cleaner's Hand Book

If you ask her, she'd tell you she was born to tidy
up a mess. She'd admit she has difficulty
lying, finding a job, and a lifetime of OCD
scrubbing ghostly footprints on polished floors.

She has a clean start — her new name
is a monosyllable with squiggles as limbs.
A simple oval shape in human form. Over the years
she doesn't add. She just wears a clean, kind smile

like her cleaner's uniform. On her wrist a pale
jade bracelet, the same good luck charm you'd bought
from your home country years ago. Imagine
what the same moustached man had said to her:

It's a sign of metaphoric richness. A luscious
green that feeds on your perfumed sweat,
a luscious green will spread wherever you are. Imagine
her paying for a metaphoric bargain that came with

extra warmth of his hand. Then, one January day
she put her hand on her heart and became
a citizen of this country you now call home.
Bleach and rubber gloves her new amulet

against the fists of years. As if reading your mind,
she lays her hand in front of you, half opened,
like a smiling lotus. You see palm lines middle age
has carved. They read like countless footnotes

on the obscure ways a story can go off its plot.
But you want to close that hand. You know those sensitive fingertips as you know your own — pricked by hope one too many times, they'll always be close to a hidden blade.

Autopsy Room

Huddled in the corner of the train
vertical in mortis rigour someone
is counting the number of chests
puffed to push sleep away. That's how
many buckets of epoxy he'll need
to wipe the walls clean of fingerprints
and expired gasping today.
But there'll be no blood spilling
nutrients like cold soup this morning.
No matted hair on dented skull.
Just a middle aged man —
his internal organs lay next to his head.
On the head his own face, mouth half-opened:

Put words in,
pour stale coffee in. The hole accepts anything
in order to continue counting — the number of
right answers left, times the number of repetition
needed...

Once there was a woman's leg
on the metal tray. He talked to it
in his ghost tongue
until water jets dissolved
the slurry seance
in the stainless steel altar.
The next day he stared at the corniced ceiling
remembering that leg. He counted soundlessly
the years needed for water to finally
wash him off the bed
so he'd know what having a life is like.

Objet Petit a

wrinkled, familiar, apologetic, such is
her fashion that dazzles   your eyes with
its odd floral pattern   a pallor you don't recognise
just like her voice   a foreign tune   or a detuned
    TV's canned harmony
her eyes don't see your backyard scenery –
        barbie smoke rising
                the flag of friendship brandishing...
her food a con/fusion   of meat that shaped like feet and feet
            that smell like   cheese.
her things are different from yours
        so she hides   what she isn't: coffee, music, colour; love   she
                puts
her automatic pencils, mis/used phrases, the   old red   coat
      in a ziplock bag   and becomes
a tunelessodorlesswinterlessfearless   woman   until

her new possessions accumulate—
made in China goods bought in Australia and born in Australia
friends dream of living by the beach   in Bali
inside the airless plastic, her old things conglomerate. A badge of
    honour
she sometimes hides
  sometimes reveals, it depends...
      you think that's good for her   but give the most
           ambivalent shrug
                         when she claims she's Aussie
                                  just like us.

The Old Herbalist's Bone Problem

For Dr. Wanling Lao

Osteoporosis.
The daughter of the herbalist
looks up the word in her iphone,
nods at the doctor, who
is reminded of a lolling head
on a mini statue he's seen
in a temple somewhere
on his holidays.

Os-te-o-po-ro-sis.
The doctor breaks the syllables
one by one for the daughter and
the herbalist again as if each
sound, properly round
and catarrhal,
can be converted
to a universal ideogram
by his authority. But the herbalist
found things she's more familiar with
inside his mouth:
his *yin yang* balance, the elements
of his *spleen*, status of his *qi*.

The doctor clears his
throat the way he was taught
when he wants to yawn.
His plosives professionally
explode like firecrackers,
awaking her distant memories.
She gazes at her own fractured tibia

glowing in white
shame on the wall as directed by his
delicate finger.

She lost her balance after
she lost her husband to cancer.
A crack in the bone is now a black
line across an infinity where
white bones gathered.
The universe had chanted with her that day:
Angelica Sinensis, Alisma, Codonopsis, Astragalus,
names of her favourite herbs
in a new language. Now she knows
pain has a sound. It's weaved
with soothing sibilances,
like a pocket full of insects,
trivial but alive —
An antithesis to his absence.

She likes the sound of assurance
in a word like "osteoporosis" too.
If she says it at home enough
times, maybe she will love
this language one day, like
a blind marriage common back in her
days. All she needs is to speak it
next to a basket of stones
he'd left her on the window sill,
to make them hum
close to her heart.

II

The ~~Unreturning~~ Boomerang

There is something I have to tell you, Emily

On the train the other day a woman about my age —
much older than you — spoke my tongue.
She asked if I could help her. What is it? I asked.
I mean, she was wearing a floral patterned shirt,
smelling of Vaseline, the kind that Father
used to rub all over my face in winter. I was no more
than 10. I have no money, she said. It's been a long time
since our city... I need a place to stay, and a job.
And I told her, just go home. Because there's no subtitles
in real life, on the train, or in the music that we often
misheard as questions that are missing a few words.
You are not going to believe this, Emily.
This woman in front of me, she starts to hum
an old song, something about a corpse white
moon; someone waiting for you to return. Her head
lowered and she rubbed her hands together,
back and forth, like a fly. She pressed the
rewind button on her walkman
again and again; she was lip syncing
Please help. Beg pardon?
This is what I want to tell you, Emily.
Understand the shame we feel in this echo —
How she was different by her clothes,
those pants that would make crackling noises
from static when you take them off after a long
futile day. Maybe you will laugh at her? Your sensitive
nose will know they all share the same stale smell from
exhaustion, sitting from seat to seat on different
trains. I understand your shame, Emily. When we
didn't know better, saying yes when we meant no,

voting no but our ballots were disqualified.
I lost my teacher and my city that same year.
I feel the same for many things, including
the language I used when they asked me
what I do for a living. There is no proper word.
My face slowly burns up. I rub my hands
like a fly, back and forth, trying to hide those things
as the train starts to move again.

Once There Was A Way To Go Back

This is not a choice. Which do you prefer, tinnitus or a jangling alarm clock at 5am?
There is no way to go back.

Splash cold water on face. Gasp yourself awake with an unrehearsed horrified look in the mirror.

Deconstruct your breakfast in twilight. Cold hands; colder and darker crumbs of leftover sleep. Add milk for curdled anxiety. Cut toasts into nano cubes then dip in a drug-level caffeinated calendar.

The morning news announces animals have turned nocturnal to avoid humans. You wake up at 4am to avoid yourself as an animal.

You curl up in the last safe space until you are pushed out of the night's womb; your eyes teary like your old dog's.

You repeat: Good Morning.

Go on. Count the homeless hair that floats past your face at Southern Cross Station.

By the ticket machine, a woman is mimicking the sound of a siren with a masked mouth; a man is counting soundlessly the faces that are wiped transparent by buckets of epoxy.

They don't know how to go back.

Those who want to prove they are alive sing a different tune of the morning — a vulgar imitation of a low note hummed in the underworld.

(Once there was a way to go back after you left for work in the morning. You needed to make sure all electrical appliances were switched off so you went back and forth from yesterday to the kitchen a thousand times. The shiny floorboards covered with muddy footprints mapping the way back.)

In your noise-cancelling headphone you hear everything: Liszt's *Consolation* / persistent ringing / the mud-filled mouths mewling behind your eardrum / the consolation of flashbacks / automatic doors whooshing open

That doesn't mean you don't try to go back. You put a sweetened plum under your tongue to remember where sweetness comes from.

Your doctor told you too much artificial happiness could cause diabetes just the same.

You have never seen a time machine or a time-card machine but you know the horror of counting time & getting paid for it. So you buy bandaids — one for the foot arch, one for below the hairline, one around the hypothalamus and rewind the birth chart.

Everyday you take the train to go back. You see heads lolling like rotten apples in each carriage, desperate for air and pesticides.

Every station has similar names. You get off anywhere when you open your eyes and see an Exit sign.

Self Portrait

i. The Exhibit

Sitting on a cosmic
fault an organic
matter at odds with its own
shape

Featuring absurdity
in human form
Half hallowed and one-
third full

An object with no
sides — a pencil-drawn
line begins in the middle
& rounds up
in an end-like
butt.

Just a small curve
that follows you.

ii. The Label

Oil on recycled
mistakes.
Anonymous. Born in 1997
in a now orphaned city.

iii. The Writing

I cross my legs
like Buddha

thoughts twirl
candy floss —
sticky, scented

scrawls wiggle
in the prosody of
blue smoke

line by line
a new page
ashes of words

settle
I look down —
grey blankness

gazing at me
like the clouds

Curriculum Vitae

At school I never quite knew what to say when asked about my father's occupation. My mother said "failed man". I'd sit on the bench and lean over the desk when he came home from work. I'd watch how he cracked a fake smile, kicked off his tired shoes and made rice steam in the overheated kitchen. Those traditional Chinese characters I was practising to write, stroke by stroke within a small square...were slowly pressing down.

Now I write my alphabets in lowercase. Small words no larger than bread crumbs fill the creases of my palm. Everyday I come home to crack open a tin of dog food and watch her shake off memories of chains and under-performance. She licks my hand for love or luck; neither has taste. But this roof is all I have to tell myself I have tried, before curling up in bed, forming a shape of some kind of character I once thought I had mastered writing.

My Three Encounters with Time

I.

Time is not an abstraction. He has the face of a donut hole. He used to sit atop my wardrobe, licking a lollipop, absorbing the only view he saw — our neighbour's lives displayed in vertical columns of concrete boxes with uniform square holes. I watched how my parents' toes stuck out of the blanket as I lit my first cigarette, how content they were as they slept. Time opened the window and escaped with the smoke. The next day, my mother discovered our only valuable in the drawer was gone, leaving behind two ragdolls that talked non-stop when left alone.

II.

Time's face appeared years later when I needed a second chance. He was drunk and showy in a flashy car. He'd become a known glutton: no concrete or steel, or any incessant haggling our city was famous for could preserve the minutes of our insignificant days. He took them all. When he saw me, he lifted his matador to cover his lopsided smile. But he returned something for me under my pillow. I put it in a jar and watched how it grew from a past longer than the present. I then filed, labelled, and archived each jar as instructed every day for a living.

III.

My parents now stand in front of their window, at eye-level with a lemon tree. From time to time they still curse Time, the small-time crook who pilfered from them. But they have lemons to preserve in a jar now. I've grown fingernails long enough to scratch one label off each day for a small dose of hope in the next. In the evenings, I go for a walk alone. I could feel the hot breath of my tireless stalker drifting in slow motion, around the slippery edge of my watch, brushing against my fingers. I stumbled once. Time's strong arm at once urges me on. His face, expressionless.

eunoia

turn the closed caption on let's read out
our improvised script my voice
only ghosts
from women and I speak
this is not a game just a
speak to me in English
practise a e i o u relax
my vocal cord vibrates with new
tame the loll of the
that confuse like life and denies (the nasal!)
in the middle, like,
raise the pitch of every last word
remember inflect when our
until the accent ascends
I aspire to speak to you

this drama
lowered (make sure)
can hear you take the lines
for the men
language lesson
(please) I need to
my facial muscles
power my teeth
tongue rehearse words
or insert “like”
of this sentence and
for every exclaim
character says “god!”
to a monosyllabic high
in a language not mine (when no one is around)

Why Micke is Every Newbie's First Desk

(According to its website, Micke is a best selling small desk at IKEA, designed to fit in any space)

Because Micke leaves home not knowing they have to give up their shape.
In the process of being reassembled they have become
something less whole and overly palpable.

Because even as an oversized Swede, Micke dreams to be a tiny fresh-out-of-the-box humanoid,
where Earth can be rescued with powerful
onomatopoeia in a two-dimensional world.

Because Micke sounds universal and is affordable like daydreams.

Because my orange Micke had made me feel welcome when I first said "Hello, Australia!"
to no one in particular
I only become lonely by myself later.

Because I wanted my words to be as colourful as Micke's glossy face, like planes of solid
sunshine even at night, like night light
frozen behind eyelids as I gently close its drawers.

Because where I came from bright orange belies quotidian aspirations:
the way white rice in a fancy rice bowl knows how
to hide its smell by being lukewarm.

Because the first time I put my notebook in the orange drawer my mother asked:

Will you write me a biography? Yes,
easy optimism breeds love in a new language

we now use to stare. Because
I still wobble from motion sickness
in slow motion which looks like a residue of excitement.

Because when I lay my head down on Micke's smoothness
I heard a sound — what's sloshing
like an ocean if not the wind
that keeps changing its mind?

(Because a poet once said nothing is sadder than a fallen
leaf that was lifted
higher than the tree
only to be found stuck in the gutter.)

Because we all know it doesn't have to be a leaf to be stuck.

Because when I lie down at night, I dream about being
disassembled back
to a perfect piece of wood.
My rings and everything, genuine; rooted.

Because for Micke, allen keys are for rewinding a sense of
belonging illustrated step-by-step in its manual.

Because Micke is built with what they can have. Their spare
parts never enough to start over.

The Shape of a House

My parents used to hold my finger
over a house in an English picture book
and said, This is a house. I never knew
if they were teaching me a new language
or how easy it was to shape a dream
with an index finger. Years later
I made a square with broken matchsticks, their ends
barely touching. My finger makes small
circles in the air mimicking
dove-grey smoke on a fictitious
suburban street lined
with childish quadrangles.
An inverted "V" for a roof,
a small three-sided rectangle on top
not fit for Santa.
Our thought bubbles redacted
by half-opened vertical blinds.
We learn to frame our space
with radio static and zigzag
lightning. They prick our fingers
but at last the house has a yellow
glow like the moon — a stage for
rehearsing happiness. At my desk
my hand traces the over-
completed shape of a childhood
geometry. It balances on a tangent
slowly retreating...
I miss everything in the old story book:
its musty smell, the happiness found
in a new language, where love and simple

sentences reside, unbound by space.

I pull out the remaining matches from the box,
wonder if there is enough
to make a pet dog.

The Five Organs

Liver / "Gone" / 肝
— the organ of blood

Liver rules the eyes —
my eyes the tiny pieces of seashells
spalled from the fragrant harbour
now dried up like salted fish
on a clothesline

"is sleeplessness
a sweet proximity to
aliveness?"
I asked the herbalist
as I placed my wrist
on the soft clothed cushion.
Her fingers on my pulse
never falter.

"Show me your tongue please."
And here goes my alternative
narrative as a storyteller.

Kidney / "Sun" / 腎
— The organ of spirit

Sometimes I hear my name on the news
(a bat echolocating on the edge of the world)

Sometime my tongue curdles in a thick coating
(paws on walls scratching for a sound)

a distant tinnitus
(a prophylactic to madness)

Somewhere
between my ears, a non-Euclidean
distance, it rings and rings
I cannot answer it —
Reigning aloneness, for the ears
that will never see each other.

Spleen / “Pei” / 脾
— the organ of transformation

Flashbacks &
ink black discharge
between your legs

staining your shoes. Recall
the goodbyes at the airport
wrench out a smile
a V made with your fingers
placed next to your face
forget the hurt
when air disappears
you cut the oxygen mask
like an umbilical cord
handed to you by a woman
who said
it was worse
giving birth to you

More discharge from
weak spleen — so sticky —
a failure to transform
guilt to love

Lungs / "Fai" / 肺
— the organ of waste

"Lungs" is a pathological homonym.
In solitude, *lung* enables — as in
you *lung* (can) hop into a pond and emerge
out of the street where you last dragged
your luggage to your 4th new home, or,
you *lung* (can) do what you *lung* (are able to) do
to do what you want to do
here. Either way,
you know lungs in the plural are needed
when you're out of breath doing all those things.
You learn that in your dialect the lungs are *fai* —
without the accurate intonation it is also a wave,
a waste, or a bedbug — nothing serious
in each breath you take or give

Heart / "Sum" / 心
— the organ of desire

The heart of my lips is shame
The heart of my navel is aimless
The heart between my brows is erasable
The heart of my femur yearns for nature
The heart of my buttock is a mint lolly
The heart of what I cannot see already happened
The heart of mystery is the winning lotto ticket
to hear God laugh.

The heart of my palm is jealous of
the heart of my fingertips who seduces time

The heart of this game
lies in its terms and conditions:
to play hide and seek, one must
hide the heart that seeks
to see with hurtful clarity.

Ms X

"She thought she could feel the impulse of her pulse."
Mary Jo Bang

is a shapeless bag of black wool
today pushing a trolley from a supermarket.
Her arm seats a toddler looking
blankly at the tattooed back of her man
bending over a baby in a pram.

Ms X is big among her gang
of quinoa, cat paws, and pearls
in her city's bubble tea. Her wallet,
beat up but loved, is exposed to prolonged
regret the morning-after too much.

A folded lotto ticket dulls the sound
of coins in her pocket. Ms X hears
only the promise of her supermarket
reward cards — every thousand
dollars spent, she saves $5
on sponsored dreams. Life

is kind to her; she just needs to
spend it. In City X, a city to be,
locals are weary of things too close
to home. But Ms X loves the corner
where she can make coffee
behind her kitchen's vertical

blinds alone. She wishes that wherever
she goes, the pram will fit the aisle between
rows of tables at the food court.

And her man is always happy
with the baby in the pram. Always –

until one day Ms X too leaves City X
and swears to be everything this city is not.
By using the reward cards that lend her life's
discounted wisdom, she'll be more, as promised
in the fine prints on the back of each lie
she's been told.

III

A ~~Lonely~~ Paper Airplane

Not Trying to Win the Archibald Prize

"She comes out of the dark seeking pie, instead finds two dead peacocks."

Diane Seuss

Every night I put up a small
exhibition of dark objects
against an empty dark window
only my black eyes can see. A flicker of street
light my golden crown.

(The spectators agree
amber lights implies accidental
voyeurism.)

I paint a woman in minimal brush
strokes
the final soft rondure — a bit too tender — the face
of her greyish elongated body below
Together, we watch the way gum tree leaves
sway like parting
lovers in the breeze; an acoustic hum,
the flirtatious spread of limbs.

She twirls towards the frame — her movements
scratch the canvas, setting aflame
every particle in the atmosphere.

But soon I realise my mistake:
watercolour hung too soon will drip
like time ill-spent. Her legs
deliquesce, staining my masterpiece
with an intense redness.

(Spectators now assume red
denotes either horror
or fortune)

In the morning moon,
curtains are opened once again
to a white wall of thick fog.
My escaping companion is now
a small shape on the edge
of my window

It resembles an arc of a pale egg
about to roll into place, open
for all to see
what searching for freedom is like.

Customer Service

First she whispers *I just want you to be happy.*
I look out the window and see the eaves-dropping
moth dripping waxy shame on our hot bare wall.

Then she takes a short course, some kind of customer
service, and gets a job. She says it's all about
experience, the '*demonstratable*' kind. I kiss her.

She rolls over, more hopeful than she'd ever be.
Soon, she learns techniques from men and women
in suits and powerful cards who assume we want

the same. *Full service means* (she swallows some saliva)
if they think they are flying, you should be the wind.
And so we learn how to be that, and metal, and fire.

But our house is always damp. Her customers come
and go like vapour. When she stands still,
I hear the trembling of her leg — a rapid vibration

of a ten-cent glued to her heel. *For good luck*,
she says. *Customers will make us right*,
I pray as my palms work to smooth the satin sheets

underneath our bodies. Clumps of old dreams
fall off. Their dull existence makes a full sound
as they collide with dusty loose change, next to

shoes, used tissues. We are mere moth specimens –
our wings pinned, fluttering; our sweat between skin
fogs the mirror above. We exhale to keep still.

I try to think of the lives cracked opened by her
luckless heels, how each swollen cockroach egg bursts –
a violence I film and sell for $10 in the darkest street.

Because love as we know it thrives in every unequal
exchange. It is the cries of all the broken carapace,
for a tiny (yet magnificent) breath we hold for each other.

Us (& That’s Why We’re All Alike)

This is a significant time for us.
We have a permanent spot to make dots
the rest of our lives. Each placement
assigned, approved, then lovelessly appraised
by the supervisor sitting behind us
who by default knows what size
and colour of dots the world needs.
At break, I sit among us — head lowered,
tongue lolled — and copy answers
for the compulsory staff survey.
Our names bilingual, we are multilingual
in saying “can”. So skilled at
putting tiny ticks in tinier boxes to agree
with our mouthful of over-chewed sandwich
we don’t need to squint our eyes to choose
the best place between __ M __ F (Tick only)
__ Married __ Single (Mandatory)
__ children __ pets __ cactuses (round
number only). We get a bonus for being
“one of us”. Like the rest of us,
I worry about the upcoming task rotation:
the corporate mechanism
to make sure we are good at part of
something (with demonstrated examples).
In this concrete box full of
dots we are paid to connect
fragments and incomplete
arcs. We get used to hugging
our belly and entertaining each other
with our favourite snacks in drawers

8 hours a day. We bond
by not asking how each of us
become the other. We ask:
Do you remember the REBEL —
The one who had once tapped on the keyboard
loudly when the boss was not around?
But the machine, banal and
philistine, only autocorrected and made copies
of copies to inauthenticate the only sound we know —
that low hum from a human-size seagull
sweating through the eye holes to win
hot chips from the easy-to-please crowd. True,
we don't need mirrors to see
sameness. We wipe our faces, rub
runny makeup of gray and moss green
to thicken our curriculum vitae year after year.
Perhaps if we'd known how to hide properly,
say, like the violinist between
these walls, selling what he has
not given up, we would've made a fortune,
found meaning in life, or at least disappeared
into a new fiction...

When Dust Falls on Our Hair

Next to the sweat
moistened bruise burgundy
bed sheet a writhing
underneath mocks
the pain you suffer.
Fast forward to 20 years
after our reincarnation –
Our tearless eyes blink
at the shivery white moon
trying to remember
our licence plate
numbers like a private joke.
The little game we used to play –
making up simple phrases
out of numbers and letters
graffitied on lamp posts.
How can you see
beauty in treacle black
A,B,C – letters of our new
language that in our previous lives
were called chicken intestines
when misspelt?
If this is 50 years later
will you still hear our hair
break from their follicles
or see the fine prints
of cause and effect on our palm lines?
Will the witty words we create
from alphabets soup
transform slime green decay, or

turbid grey sewage slop that is
the anatomy of a leaky old body?
Inside the harmless muscle
there're nerves, nerves
flower itch. Itch seeds a pain.
It's the unhappy laughter
your brain orders
the body to make
at 3am as our window becomes
varicose blue, sleepless
orange, liver spots brown.
Next to me, wet silvery
breaths shatter
a putrid silence. When a hand
brushes a stray hair
out of your glassy
face, I notice it is just
my old, lingering claw
falling off the edge
of the bed.

How to Run Away (& be a Glowing Shadow Anime-styled)

Heaven spins an inverted zentangle in blue after 5.
The nether labyrinths unfurl their furry edges
and twirl
to the rhythm of dancing Hiragana.
Stale office workers go after hyper
animated ellipses
like perverted pac-man after his dots.
Escaped bored mannequins still on the run bang
their cotton fists at vending machines
for an analgesic that relieves mild symptoms of
banal lovesickness.
I get on my spaceship to outrun men
and women in their flashy blue suits
with XL belt buckle
to reach Yuriko...
Hoodlums guard their street corners with sharpened
jawlines – So sharp
even Time bleeds
when passing them by.
So sharp, even Tomorrow is shredded
into a puddle of worms,
spreading like a heartless
paste that no one misses.

On the platform, people hold their breath
for the last train. Their left
hand touches their right for cheap comfort.
I stand on the platform and wait for Yuriko
to glow in LED

to swallow the last of my
etiolated shadow in her windy embrace.
Heart-shaped syllables, bold, italicised
clinking out of her dimples. I
repeat what she says — each mispronunciation
a deliberate slip of the tongue
deep into the lighted ad box
(where love is 15 seconds long).
Our breaths hot and fast like exciting metaphor
never captured by the script they make her read.
Outside, neon lights dart through our
translucent arms like possessed
toy trains stuck in infinite loops.
I kill them like lights are killed.

In darkness we hug till we're warm and bright.

The Fire Eater

(Inspired by the Fireballs on the banks of the Yarra River)

Someone has to do it. Someone has to dive
into the sewage in the city's heart
to remove debris of dead relationships.
Someone will have to hold
breath and wade through tarry stool
gritting teeth against the bitter iron taste,
and suppress the urge
to write a poem about it. Someone at the circus
will have to make a call to strangers
8 hours a day, while someone has to be an aerialist
trembling with fear of height and
linearity. Someone will sleep
knowing they will never be
the one to ride a unicycle
towards the ceiling, or to fly across
eaves of garrets and penthouses
with arms spread. At night, someone
has to hunt with a can of Coke
filled with alcohol poured from discarded
liquor bottles, ready to spit fire into the cloudless sky.

Everyday you eat fire in order to spit fire to build
hope and believe in the good intention of smoke –
fireballs shoot up from the tower to illuminate
those who stay behind and choose to endure
tear gas disguised as smog. You choose to leave
and speak another language in the fire
spitting city such as this one; to be
an acrobat leaping to hang a star in the sky.
Someone will have to look up

and wait for you to fall
to complete the cycle;
to see how the fire
eats the star
while making
as little sound
as possible

Self Portrait as a Rubber Chicken

I consider myself an everyone must-have.
See this mouth that cannot chew
on these hand-like claws? In it my best
answer to life's laughless tickles.

I got arms that flap like a peace-spreading
dove when played with; always try to grab
or clap when I found meaning. If I have
feet, they are only there to mock other chickens

who run. Oh, I don't have feathers.
Feathers hide too many secrets. I have my
goosebumps like open sores, each an open-ended
story and each has you in it. At the shop I hang

like a bright yellow exclamation mark to dramatise
your entrance. When you approach, I fill
my entire inside with intestines so you can watch
as my eyes pop straight into a viscous future —

Through a hole I don't know I have
comes a sound. I want it to sound deep,
to mimic the critical moment of growing up
overnight, but I can never decide

if I should laugh or cry afterwards.
I remember your eyes as you leave —
round and astounded, not unlike mine.
In them the very potential to be trypophiliac.

You'll savour the squeeze of my body too,
one that gave me the wide-eyed chicken look before
you fled. Soon you'll see the same face
in the mirror every morning. Your hands will flap

& clap as if they won't stop growing. The sound
they make barely enough to cover up
the mirror breaking squeak from your mouth,
reminding you of me, still hanging like a !

In the End I Did Not Become a Beast

nor have I played the guitar on stage
wooing the crowd with an accent
that is meant for a themeless song.

In the end I only write and paint
like a child the things I want to do
to your body. I use them to bargain

with a vending machine for a soft
heart soaked in love, then hide it from
you like a criminal in a Higashino suspense.

Once I trained my dog to be a fortune teller.
When the time comes, she'd show me in urine text
the sideway columns of your thoughts

such as: what if we have love? The answer
will appear like a new horoscope
under the pornographic home of stars.

And like smoke, we'll intertwine into the next
three lives. I'll fondle the sensual faux fur
underneath your breath until you say "stop"

and slap my arm, your face only half-turned...

You must admit, it takes a real romantic to accept
the power of *cannot not be* and double deny
the doom of fantasy with no window to break...

Stagnant dreams blossom cliches that cling-
wrap my skin like badly scripted scenes.
In the end I only manage to maul these lines

into unmelodious coughs for the crowd.
Such an ageing non-beast me, to have to bend
slowly for a sob. Love (and you) — a beauty not

untrue, even as I have to make it up in a poem.

God's Reality Show

After 5pm God puts on his sunglasses
to watch his creatures in a low budget reality show.
It opens with synchronised
bodies on scene-less streets. He watches
spindly legs run from rat tails on rain splattered
shoes, from white lights, mean mouths, and scented
kleenex flying in dusk-heavy rain. Someone's
always screaming, a sound that resonates
with the way air particles shatter, or casualties
of raindrops on rooftop. This is no child's
nightmare and we're all in it.
I am one of God's less favourite characters.
Everyday I rehearse the only line in my script:
We'll make it to Friday again in a tone that mimics
a paper cup crushed by lack of space in a closing hand.
Everyday I repeat one thing — to push minutes
second by second doggy-styled
from the ocean of time as I hide
blood and vomit with dirt for the Top Ten.
Our armpits where wings never grow
smell of wet dog fur in a plastic bag
after 5. Even cats and ants run from the avalanche of time
I've piled up during the day. We take a selfie
to remember our face
and follow the feet
in front of us, armed
with only a protective incantation
to reach the other side. No one burns
paper money or houses for our souls;
no one scatters rice and mumble:

go on, don't look back, go...
as we walk by.
I cross the intersection without reincarnation.
On the train I catch a glimpse of God's curls
and his dice cup before faint light of houses
comes on. Before darkness descends on all windows.
Before their cold surface
once again reflects our hollow cheek
bones and aching elbows, uselessly bunched
side by side, exhausted, one carriage
after another, against the coming of the next day.
Before God yawns
and switches off his TV.

Appendix

Ten Unscientific Facts about Poets Who Write in a Ghost Tongue

1. A non-native English speaking migrant is not redundant like koala bears or tuna fish. But do not confuse them with the species "expats". They are "different", for reasons still unknown.

2. Migrant poets get used to the heavy whiteness of daytime by making their eyes glass-like. So they can see ghosts, in an unintrusive font.

3. The dissonant sound you hear when a migrant-poet speaks is caused by a molecular collision during the busy reshuffling of nouns, verbs, conditions, suppositions in a hollowed out ideogram. Ear phones do not help.

4. A typical migrant travels 8,497,605.10 kilometres to become a poet, an average of 50.28 footsteps per word, including backtracking. Scientists sometimes use these footprints to measure the size of the world, without giving these poets credits.

5. Migrant/poets are spoiled by the fragrance of their well-fermented home songs. Some may attempt to translate the lyrics to an olfactory language they call their *ghost tongue.*

6. When we migrant (poets) first meet a polysyllabic word we give it new meaning by getting to know its taste in love. We study the blind marriages between their consonants and vowels. We pronounce them and imagine what they sound like when they are (heart) broken. That's why most of us are sensitive to what people think of our English.

7. At least one migrant/poet is polyphasic. He masticates every new vocab as if it were an overcooked intestine from a book. But some are just indigestible. In that case, he regurgitates them into unsolvable anagrams.

8. Almost all (migrant) poets use their special skills to pay bills. Some are able to create a vibration that resembles a rumble in the air with the effect of Delta Wave. It helps insomniacs to sleep. Talented (migrant) poets like these are much sought after in the black market.

9. To write in a non-native language, some migrant-poets develop their own techniques over time. They mutter on their way to bed at night for their ancestors' blessings. They're often surprised when words wiggle out of their mouths or fingertips like incense smoke.

10. Migrantpoets are common extra-terrestrial mammals. To make themselves heard, they hiss, croak, kiss, croon, groan, wet their lips until a deep longing surges and vibrates the vocal cord. Some succeed eventually to create a fictional thunder in an ink storm.

Previous Publications

Some of the poems included in this book have previously appeared in the following publications:

Peril Magazine: "Don't Give the Lazy Immigrant Flowers"
Mascara Literary Review: "Hard to Think", "Rooftop Chicken (Fiction of Flying)"
Cordite: "On Post-Victory Day"
Voice & Verse Poetry Magazine: "There's something I have to tell you, Emily..."
Gargouille: "eunoia"
Ucity Review: "The Shape of a House", "The Fire Eater"
The Suburban Review: "Us"
Oystercatcher One: 101 Poems (5 Islands Press, 2024): "Why Micke is Every Newbie's First Desk"

The original version of "God's Reality Show" was a finalist in the 2019 MPU International Poetry Competition.

www.ingramcontent.com/pod-product-compliance
Ingram Content Group Australia Pty Ltd
76 Discovery Rd, Dandenong South VIC 3175, AU
AUHW021009050326
424219AU00001B/312

9 781923 099647